Cake Order

INFORMATION

NAME

COMPANY

ADDRESS

E-MAIL ADDRESS

WEBSITE

PHONE   **FAX**

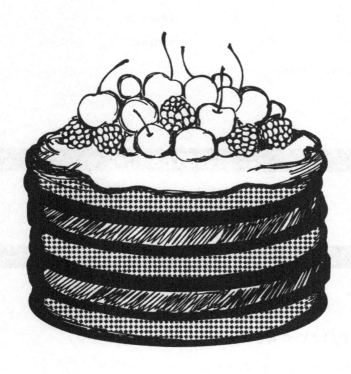

Cake Order Book

ORDER NUMBER .... ORDER DATE ....

PICKUP ☐   DELIVERY ☐   DELIVERY DATE ....

CUSTOMER DETAILS

NAME ....

ADDRESS ....

PHONE NUMBER ....

E-MAIL ....

CAKE DETAILS

CAKE TYPE .... **TIER** ....

QUANTIFY .... **CAKE SIZE** ....

FLAVOR .... **SHAPE** ....

COLOR SCHEME .... **FROSTING** ....

FILLING .... **WRITING** ....

SPECIAL INSTRUCTIONS ....

....

....

NOTES

....

....

....

PAYMENT DETAILS

TOTAL COST .... **DEPOSIT PAID** .... **TOTAL PAID** ....

FORM OF PAYMENT ....

Cake Order Book

DESIGN

Cake Order Book

ORDER NUMBER

ORDER DATE

PICKUP ☐   DELIVERY ☐

DELIVERY DATE

CUSTOMER DETAILS

NAME ....

ADDRESS ....

PHONE NUMBER ....

E-MAIL ....

CAKE DETAILS

CAKE TYPE ....   TIER ....

QUANTIFY ....   CAKE SIZE ....

FLAVOR ....   SHAPE ....

COLOR SCHEME ....   FROSTING ....

FILLING ....   WRITING ....

SPECIAL INSTRUCTIONS ....

....

....

NOTES

....

....

....

PAYMENT DETAILS

TOTAL COST ....   DEPOSIT PAID ....   TOTAL PAID ....

FORM OF PAYMENT ....

Cake Order Book

DESIGN

Cake Order Book

ORDER NUMBER _____   ORDER DATE _____

PICKUP ☐   DELIVERY ☐   DELIVERY DATE _____

CUSTOMER DETAILS

NAME ....

ADDRESS ....

PHONE NUMBER ....

E-MAIL ....

CAKE DETAILS

CAKE TYPE ....   TIER ....

QUANTIFY ....   CAKE SIZE ....

FLAVOR ....   SHAPE ....

COLOR SCHEME ....   FROSTING ....

FILLING ....   WRITING ....

SPECIAL INSTRUCTIONS ....

....

....

NOTES

....
....
....

PAYMENT DETAILS

TOTAL COST ....   DEPOSIT PAID ....   TOTAL PAID ....

FORM OF PAYMENT ....

Cake Order Book

DESIGN

....

....

....

....

....

....

....

....

....

....

....

Cake Order Book

ORDER NUMBER   ORDER DATE

PICKUP ☐   DELIVERY ☐   DELIVERY DATE

CUSTOMER DETAILS

NAME ....

ADDRESS ....

PHONE NUMBER ....

E-MAIL ....

CAKE DETAILS

CAKE TYPE ....   TIER ....

QUANTIFY ....   CAKE SIZE ....

FLAVOR ....   SHAPE ....

COLOR SCHEME ....   FROSTING ....

FILLING ....   WRITING ....

SPECIAL INSTRUCTIONS ....

....

....

NOTES

....
....
....

PAYMENT DETAILS

TOTAL   DEPOSIT   TOTAL
COST ....   PAID ....   PAID ....

FORM OF PAYMENT ....

Cake Order Book

DESIGN

....
....
....
....
....
....
....
....
....
....
....

Cake Order Book

ORDER NUMBER   ORDER DATE

PICKUP ☐   DELIVERY ☐   DELIVERY DATE

CUSTOMER DETAILS

NAME ....

ADDRESS ....

PHONE NUMBER ....

E-MAIL ....

CAKE DETAILS

CAKE TYPE .... TIER ....

QUANTIFY .... CAKE SIZE ....

FLAVOR .... SHAPE ....

COLOR SCHEME .... FROSTING ....

FILLING .... WRITING ....

SPECIAL INSTRUCTIONS ....

....

....

NOTES

....

....

....

PAYMENT DETAILS

TOTAL   DEPOSIT   TOTAL

COST ....   PAID ....   PAID ....

FORM OF PAYMENT ....

Cake Order Book

DESIGN

....
....
....
....
....
....
....
....
....
....
....

Cake Order Book

ORDER NUMBER .... ORDER DATE ....

PICKUP ☐ DELIVERY ☐ DELIVERY DATE ....

CUSTOMER DETAILS

NAME ....

ADDRESS ....

PHONE NUMBER ....

E-MAIL ....

CAKE DETAILS

CAKE TYPE .... TIER ....

QUANTIFY .... CAKE SIZE ....

FLAVOR .... SHAPE ....

COLOR SCHEME .... FROSTING ....

FILLING .... WRITING ....

SPECIAL INSTRUCTIONS ....

....

....

NOTES

....

....

....

PAYMENT DETAILS

TOTAL COST .... DEPOSIT PAID .... TOTAL PAID ....

FORM OF PAYMENT ....

Cake Order Book

DESIGN

....
....
....
....
....
....
....
....
....
....
....

Cake Order Book

ORDER NUMBER .... ORDER DATE ....

PICKUP ☐   DELIVERY ☐   DELIVERY DATE

CUSTOMER DETAILS

NAME ....

ADDRESS ....

PHONE NUMBER ....

E-MAIL ....

CAKE DETAILS

CAKE TYPE .... TIER ....

QUANTIFY .... CAKE SIZE ....

FLAVOR .... SHAPE ....

COLOR SCHEME .... FROSTING ....

FILLING .... WRITING ....

SPECIAL INSTRUCTIONS ....

....

....

NOTES

....

....

....

PAYMENT DETAILS

TOTAL COST ....   DEPOSIT PAID ....   TOTAL PAID ....

FORM OF PAYMENT ....

Cake Order Book

DESIGN

Cake Order Book

ORDER NUMBER .... ORDER DATE ....

PICKUP ☐   DELIVERY ☐   DELIVERY DATE ....

CUSTOMER DETAILS

NAME ....

ADDRESS ....

PHONE NUMBER ....

E-MAIL ....

CAKE DETAILS

CAKE TYPE .... TIER ....

QUANTIFY .... CAKE SIZE ....

FLAVOR .... SHAPE ....

COLOR SCHEME .... FROSTING ....

FILLING .... WRITING ....

SPECIAL INSTRUCTIONS ....

....

....

NOTES

....

....

....

PAYMENT DETAILS

TOTAL COST .... DEPOSIT PAID .... TOTAL PAID ....

FORM OF PAYMENT ....

Cake Order Book

DESIGN

Cake Order Book

ORDER NUMBER .... ORDER DATE ....

PICKUP ☐   DELIVERY ☐   DELIVERY DATE ....

CUSTOMER DETAILS

NAME ....

ADDRESS ....

PHONE NUMBER ....

E-MAIL ....

CAKE DETAILS

CAKE TYPE .... TIER ....

QUANTIFY .... CAKE SIZE ....

FLAVOR .... SHAPE ....

COLOR SCHEME .... FROSTING ....

FILLING .... WRITING ....

SPECIAL INSTRUCTIONS ....

....

....

NOTES

....

....

....

PAYMENT DETAILS

TOTAL COST ....   DEPOSIT PAID ....   TOTAL PAID ....

FORM OF PAYMENT ....

Cake Order Book

DESIGN

....

....

....

....

....

....

....

....

....

....

....

Cake Order Book

ORDER NUMBER   ORDER DATE

PICKUP ☐   DELIVERY ☐   DELIVERY DATE

CUSTOMER DETAILS

NAME ....

ADDRESS ....

PHONE NUMBER ....

E-MAIL ....

CAKE DETAILS

CAKE TYPE ....   TIER ....

QUANTIFY ....   CAKE SIZE ....

FLAVOR ....   SHAPE ....

COLOR SCHEME ....   FROSTING ....

FILLING ....   WRITING ....

SPECIAL INSTRUCTIONS ....

....

....

NOTES

....
....
....

PAYMENT DETAILS

TOTAL   DEPOSIT   TOTAL
COST ....   PAID ....   PAID ....

FORM OF PAYMENT ....

Cake Order Book

DESIGN

Cake Order Book

ORDER NUMBER .... ORDER DATE ....

PICKUP ☐ DELIVERY ☐ DELIVERY DATE ....

CUSTOMER DETAILS

NAME ....

ADDRESS ....

PHONE NUMBER ....

E-MAIL ....

CAKE DETAILS

CAKE TYPE .... TIER ....

QUANTIFY .... CAKE SIZE ....

FLAVOR .... SHAPE ....

COLOR SCHEME .... FROSTING ....

FILLING .... WRITING ....

SPECIAL INSTRUCTIONS ....

....

....

NOTES

....

....

....

PAYMENT DETAILS

TOTAL COST .... DEPOSIT PAID .... TOTAL PAID ....

FORM OF PAYMENT ....

Cake Order Book

DESIGN

....

....

....

....

....

....

....

....

....

....

....

Cake Order Book

ORDER NUMBER   ORDER DATE

PICKUP ☐   DELIVERY ☐   DELIVERY DATE

CUSTOMER DETAILS

NAME ....

ADDRESS ....

PHONE NUMBER ....

E-MAIL ....

CAKE DETAILS

CAKE TYPE .... TIER ....

QUANTIFY .... CAKE SIZE ....

FLAVOR .... SHAPE ....

COLOR SCHEME .... FROSTING ....

FILLING .... WRITING ....

SPECIAL INSTRUCTIONS ....

....

....

NOTES

....

....

....

PAYMENT DETAILS

TOTAL COST	DEPOSIT PAID	TOTAL PAID
....	....	....

FORM OF PAYMENT ....

Cake Order Book

Cake Order Book

ORDER NUMBER   ORDER DATE

PICKUP ☐   DELIVERY ☐   DELIVERY DATE

CUSTOMER DETAILS

NAME ....

ADDRESS ....

PHONE NUMBER ....

E-MAIL ....

CAKE DETAILS

CAKE TYPE ....   TIER ....

QUANTIFY ....   CAKE SIZE ....

FLAVOR ....   SHAPE ....

COLOR SCHEME ....   FROSTING ....

FILLING ....   WRITING ....

SPECIAL INSTRUCTIONS ....

....

....

NOTES

....

....

....

PAYMENT DETAILS

TOTAL   DEPOSIT   TOTAL

COST ....   PAID ....   PAID ....

FORM OF PAYMENT ....

Cake Order Book

DESIGN

....
....
....
....
....
....
....
....
....
....

Cake Order Book

ORDER NUMBER .... ORDER DATE ....

PICKUP ☐   DELIVERY ☐   DELIVERY DATE

CUSTOMER DETAILS

NAME ....

ADDRESS ....

PHONE NUMBER ....

E-MAIL ....

CAKE DETAILS

CAKE TYPE .... TIER ....

QUANTIFY .... CAKE SIZE ....

FLAVOR .... SHAPE ....

COLOR SCHEME .... FROSTING ....

FILLING .... WRITING ....

SPECIAL INSTRUCTIONS ....

....

....

NOTES

....
....
....

PAYMENT DETAILS

TOTAL   DEPOSIT   TOTAL
COST ....   PAID ....   PAID ....

FORM OF PAYMENT ....

Cake Order Book

DESIGN

....
....
....
....
....
....
....
....
....
....
....
....

Cake Order Book

ORDER NUMBER .... ORDER DATE ....

PICKUP ☐   DELIVERY ☐   DELIVERY DATE ....

CUSTOMER DETAILS

NAME ....

ADDRESS ....

PHONE NUMBER ....

E-MAIL ....

CAKE DETAILS

CAKE TYPE .... TIER ....

QUANTIFY .... CAKE SIZE ....

FLAVOR .... SHAPE ....

COLOR SCHEME .... FROSTING ....

FILLING .... WRITING ....

SPECIAL INSTRUCTIONS ....

....

....

NOTES

....

....

....

PAYMENT DETAILS

TOTAL COST ....   DEPOSIT PAID ....   TOTAL PAID ....

FORM OF PAYMENT ....

Cake Order Book

DESIGN

Cake Order Book

ORDER NUMBER .... ORDER DATE ....

PICKUP ☐ DELIVERY ☐ DELIVERY DATE

CUSTOMER DETAILS

NAME ....

ADDRESS ....

PHONE NUMBER ....

E-MAIL ....

CAKE DETAILS

CAKE TYPE .... TIER ....

QUANTIFY .... CAKE SIZE ....

FLAVOR .... SHAPE ....

COLOR SCHEME .... FROSTING ....

FILLING .... WRITING ....

SPECIAL INSTRUCTIONS ....

....

....

NOTES

....

....

....

PAYMENT DETAILS

TOTAL COST .... DEPOSIT PAID .... TOTAL PAID ....

FORM OF PAYMENT ....

Cake Order Book

DESIGN

....

....

....

....

....

....

....

....

....

....

....

Cake Order Book

ORDER NUMBER   ORDER DATE

PICKUP ☐   DELIVERY ☐   DELIVERY DATE

CUSTOMER DETAILS

NAME ....

ADDRESS ....

PHONE NUMBER ....

E-MAIL ....

CAKE DETAILS

CAKE TYPE ....   TIER ....

QUANTIFY ....   CAKE SIZE ....

FLAVOR ....   SHAPE ....

COLOR SCHEME ....   FROSTING ....

FILLING ....   WRITING ....

SPECIAL INSTRUCTIONS ....

....

....

NOTES

....

....

....

PAYMENT DETAILS

TOTAL   DEPOSIT   TOTAL
   COST ....   PAID ....   PAID ....

FORM OF PAYMENT ....

Cake Order Book

DESIGN

....

....

....

....

....

....

....

....

....

....

....

Cake Order Book

ORDER NUMBER .... ORDER DATE ....

PICKUP ☐   DELIVERY ☐   DELIVERY DATE

CUSTOMER DETAILS

NAME ....

ADDRESS ....

PHONE NUMBER ....

E-MAIL ....

CAKE DETAILS

CAKE TYPE .... TIER ....

QUANTIFY .... CAKE SIZE ....

FLAVOR .... SHAPE ....

COLOR SCHEME .... FROSTING ....

FILLING .... WRITING ....

SPECIAL INSTRUCTIONS ....

....

....

NOTES

....
....
....

PAYMENT DETAILS

TOTAL COST	DEPOSIT PAID	TOTAL PAID
....	....	....

FORM OF PAYMENT ....

Cake Order Book

DESIGN

....
....
....
....
....
....
....
....
....
....
....

Cake Order Book

ORDER NUMBER   ORDER DATE

PICKUP ☐   DELIVERY ☐   DELIVERY DATE

CUSTOMER DETAILS

NAME ....

ADDRESS ....

PHONE NUMBER ....

E-MAIL ....

CAKE DETAILS

CAKE TYPE ....   TIER ....

QUANTIFY ....   CAKE SIZE ....

FLAVOR ....   SHAPE ....

COLOR SCHEME ....   FROSTING ....

FILLING ....   WRITING ....

SPECIAL INSTRUCTIONS ....

....

....

NOTES

....

....

....

PAYMENT DETAILS

TOTAL COST ....   DEPOSIT PAID ....   TOTAL PAID ....

FORM OF PAYMENT ....

Cake Order Book

DESIGN

....
....
....
....
....
....
....
....
....
....
....

Cake Order Book

ORDER NUMBER .... ORDER DATE ....

PICKUP ☐   DELIVERY ☐   DELIVERY DATE

CUSTOMER DETAILS

NAME ....

ADDRESS ....

PHONE NUMBER ....

E-MAIL ....

CAKE DETAILS

CAKE TYPE .... TIER ....

QUANTIFY .... CAKE SIZE ....

FLAVOR .... SHAPE ....

COLOR SCHEME .... FROSTING ....

FILLING .... WRITING ....

SPECIAL INSTRUCTIONS ....

....

....

NOTES

....

....

....

PAYMENT DETAILS

TOTAL COST ....   DEPOSIT PAID ....   TOTAL PAID ....

FORM OF PAYMENT ....

Cake Order Book

DESIGN

....

....

....

....

....

....

....

....

....

....

....

....

Cake Order Book

ORDER NUMBER   ORDER DATE

PICKUP ☐   DELIVERY ☐   DELIVERY DATE

CUSTOMER DETAILS

NAME ....

ADDRESS ....

PHONE NUMBER ....

E-MAIL ....

CAKE DETAILS

CAKE TYPE .... TIER ....

QUANTIFY .... CAKE SIZE ....

FLAVOR .... SHAPE ....

COLOR SCHEME .... FROSTING ....

FILLING .... WRITING ....

SPECIAL INSTRUCTIONS ....

....

....

NOTES

....
....
....

PAYMENT DETAILS

TOTAL   DEPOSIT   TOTAL
COST .... PAID ....   PAID ....

FORM OF PAYMENT ....

Cake Order Book

DESIGN

....
....
....
....
....
....
....
....
....
....
....

Cake Order Book

ORDER NUMBER   ORDER DATE

PICKUP ☐   DELIVERY ☐   DELIVERY DATE

CUSTOMER DETAILS

NAME ....

ADDRESS ....

PHONE NUMBER ....

E-MAIL ....

CAKE DETAILS

CAKE TYPE ....   TIER ....

QUANTIFY ....   CAKE SIZE ....

FLAVOR ....   SHAPE ....

COLOR SCHEME ....   FROSTING ....

FILLING ....   WRITING ....

SPECIAL INSTRUCTIONS ....

....

....

NOTES

....
....
....

PAYMENT DETAILS

TOTAL   DEPOSIT   TOTAL
COST ....   PAID ....   PAID ....

FORM OF PAYMENT ....

Cake Order Book

Cake Order Book

ORDER NUMBER .... ORDER DATE ....

PICKUP ☐   DELIVERY ☐   DELIVERY DATE ....

CUSTOMER DETAILS

NAME ....

ADDRESS ....

PHONE NUMBER ....

E-MAIL ....

CAKE DETAILS

CAKE TYPE .... TIER ....

QUANTIFY .... CAKE SIZE ....

FLAVOR .... SHAPE ....

COLOR SCHEME .... FROSTING ....

FILLING .... WRITING ....

SPECIAL INSTRUCTIONS ....

....

....

NOTES

....

....

....

PAYMENT DETAILS

TOTAL   DEPOSIT   TOTAL

COST .... PAID .... PAID ....

FORM OF PAYMENT ....

Cake Order Book

DESIGN

....
....
....
....
....
....
....
....
....
....
....

Cake Order Book

ORDER NUMBER   ORDER DATE

PICKUP ☐   DELIVERY ☐   DELIVERY DATE

CUSTOMER DETAILS

NAME ....

ADDRESS ....

PHONE NUMBER ....

E-MAIL ....

CAKE DETAILS

CAKE TYPE ....   TIER ....

QUANTIFY ....   CAKE SIZE ....

FLAVOR ....   SHAPE ....

COLOR SCHEME ....   FROSTING ....

FILLING ....   WRITING ....

SPECIAL INSTRUCTIONS ....

....

....

NOTES

....

....

....

PAYMENT DETAILS

TOTAL   DEPOSIT   TOTAL
COST ....   PAID ....   PAID ....

FORM OF PAYMENT ....

Cake Order Book

DESIGN

....
....
....
....
....
....
....
....
....
....
....
....
....
....

Cake Order Book

ORDER NUMBER .... ORDER DATE ....

PICKUP ☐   DELIVERY ☐   DELIVERY DATE

CUSTOMER DETAILS

NAME ....

ADDRESS ....

PHONE NUMBER ....

E-MAIL ....

CAKE DETAILS

CAKE TYPE ....   TIER ....

QUANTIFY ....   CAKE SIZE ....

FLAVOR ....   SHAPE ....

COLOR SCHEME ....   FROSTING ....

FILLING ....   WRITING ....

SPECIAL INSTRUCTIONS ....

....

....

NOTES

....
....
....

PAYMENT DETAILS

TOTAL COST ....   DEPOSIT PAID ....   TOTAL PAID ....

FORM OF PAYMENT ....

Cake Order Book

DESIGN

Cake Order Book

ORDER NUMBER | ORDER DATE

PICKUP ☐   DELIVERY ☐   DELIVERY DATE

CUSTOMER DETAILS

NAME ....

ADDRESS ....

PHONE NUMBER ....

E-MAIL ....

CAKE DETAILS

CAKE TYPE ....   TIER ....

QUANTIFY ....   CAKE SIZE ....

FLAVOR ....   SHAPE ....

COLOR SCHEME ....   FROSTING ....

FILLING ....   WRITING ....

SPECIAL INSTRUCTIONS ....

....

....

NOTES

....

....

....

PAYMENT DETAILS

TOTAL   DEPOSIT   TOTAL

COST ....   PAID ....   PAID ....

FORM OF PAYMENT ....

Cake Order Book

DESIGN

....
....
....
....
....
....
....
....
....
....
....

Cake Order Book

ORDER NUMBER .... ORDER DATE ....

PICKUP ☐   DELIVERY ☐   DELIVERY DATE ....

CUSTOMER DETAILS

NAME ....

ADDRESS ....

PHONE NUMBER ....

E-MAIL ....

CAKE DETAILS

CAKE TYPE .... **TIER** ....

QUANTIFY .... **CAKE SIZE** ....

FLAVOR .... **SHAPE** ....

COLOR SCHEME .... **FROSTING** ....

FILLING .... **WRITING** ....

SPECIAL INSTRUCTIONS ....

....

....

NOTES

....

....

....

PAYMENT DETAILS

TOTAL COST .... **DEPOSIT PAID** .... **TOTAL PAID** ....

FORM OF PAYMENT ....

Cake Order Book

....

....

....

....

....

....

....

....

....

....

....

Cake Order Book

ORDER NUMBER .... ORDER DATE ....

PICKUP ☐   DELIVERY ☐   DELIVERY DATE

CUSTOMER DETAILS

NAME ....

ADDRESS ....

PHONE NUMBER ....

E-MAIL ....

CAKE DETAILS

CAKE TYPE .... **TIER** ....

QUANTIFY .... **CAKE SIZE** ....

FLAVOR .... **SHAPE** ....

COLOR SCHEME .... **FROSTING** ....

FILLING .... **WRITING** ....

SPECIAL INSTRUCTIONS ....

....

....

NOTES

....

....

....

PAYMENT DETAILS

TOTAL COST .... **DEPOSIT PAID** .... **TOTAL PAID** ....

FORM OF PAYMENT ....

Cake Order Book

DESIGN

....
....
....
....
....
....
....
....
....
....
....
....

Cake Order Book

ORDER NUMBER   ORDER DATE

PICKUP ☐   DELIVERY ☐   DELIVERY DATE

CUSTOMER DETAILS

NAME ....

ADDRESS ....

PHONE NUMBER ....

E-MAIL ....

CAKE DETAILS

CAKE TYPE .... TIER ....

QUANTIFY .... CAKE SIZE ....

FLAVOR .... SHAPE ....

COLOR SCHEME .... FROSTING ....

FILLING .... WRITING ....

SPECIAL INSTRUCTIONS ....

....

....

NOTES

....

....

....

PAYMENT DETAILS

TOTAL   DEPOSIT   TOTAL
COST ....   PAID ....   PAID ....

FORM OF PAYMENT ....

Cake Order Book

DESIGN

....

....

....

....

....

....

....

....

....

....

Cake Order Book

ORDER NUMBER .... **ORDER DATE** ....

PICKUP ☐   **DELIVERY** ☐   **DELIVERY DATE** ....

CUSTOMER DETAILS

NAME ....

ADDRESS ....

PHONE NUMBER ....

E-MAIL ....

CAKE DETAILS

CAKE TYPE .... **TIER** ....

QUANTIFY .... **CAKE SIZE** ....

FLAVOR .... **SHAPE** ....

COLOR SCHEME .... **FROSTING** ....

FILLING .... **WRITING** ....

SPECIAL INSTRUCTIONS ....

....

....

NOTES

....

....

....

PAYMENT DETAILS

TOTAL COST ....   **DEPOSIT PAID** ....   **TOTAL PAID** ....

FORM OF PAYMENT ....

Cake Order Book

....
....
....
....
....
....
....
....
....
....
....

Cake Order Book

ORDER NUMBER .... ORDER DATE ....

PICKUP ☐   DELIVERY ☐   DELIVERY DATE ....

CUSTOMER DETAILS

NAME ....

ADDRESS ....

PHONE NUMBER ....

E-MAIL ....

CAKE DETAILS

CAKE TYPE ....   TIER ....

QUANTIFY ....   CAKE SIZE ....

FLAVOR ....   SHAPE ....

COLOR SCHEME ....   FROSTING ....

FILLING ....   WRITING ....

SPECIAL INSTRUCTIONS ....

....

....

NOTES

....

....

....

PAYMENT DETAILS

TOTAL   DEPOSIT   TOTAL
COST ....   PAID ....   PAID ....

FORM OF PAYMENT ....

Cake Order Book

DESIGN

Cake Order Book

ORDER NUMBER .... ORDER DATE ....

PICKUP ☐   DELIVERY ☐   DELIVERY DATE

CUSTOMER DETAILS

NAME ....

ADDRESS ....

PHONE NUMBER ....

E-MAIL ....

CAKE DETAILS

CAKE TYPE ....   TIER ....

QUANTIFY ....   CAKE SIZE ....

FLAVOR ....   SHAPE ....

COLOR SCHEME ....   FROSTING ....

FILLING ....   WRITING ....

SPECIAL INSTRUCTIONS ....

....

....

NOTES

....

....

....

PAYMENT DETAILS

TOTAL COST	DEPOSIT PAID	TOTAL PAID
....	....	....

FORM OF PAYMENT ....

Cake Order Book

DESIGN

Cake Order Book

ORDER NUMBER .... ORDER DATE ....

PICKUP ☐   DELIVERY ☐   DELIVERY DATE

CUSTOMER DETAILS

NAME ....

ADDRESS ....

PHONE NUMBER ....

E-MAIL ....

CAKE DETAILS

CAKE TYPE .... TIER ....

QUANTIFY .... CAKE SIZE ....

FLAVOR .... SHAPE ....

COLOR SCHEME .... FROSTING ....

FILLING .... WRITING ....

SPECIAL INSTRUCTIONS ....

....

....

NOTES

....

....

....

PAYMENT DETAILS

TOTAL   DEPOSIT   TOTAL

COST ....   PAID ....   PAID ....

FORM OF PAYMENT ....

Cake Order Book

....
....
....
....
....
....
....
....
....
....
....

Cake Order Book

ORDER NUMBER .... ORDER DATE ....

PICKUP ☐   DELIVERY ☐   DELIVERY DATE

CUSTOMER DETAILS

NAME ....

ADDRESS ....

PHONE NUMBER ....

E-MAIL ....

CAKE DETAILS

CAKE TYPE .... TIER ....

QUANTIFY .... CAKE SIZE ....

FLAVOR .... SHAPE ....

COLOR SCHEME .... FROSTING ....

FILLING .... WRITING ....

SPECIAL INSTRUCTIONS ....

....

....

NOTES

....

....

....

PAYMENT DETAILS

TOTAL COST ....   DEPOSIT PAID ....   TOTAL PAID ....

FORM OF PAYMENT ....

Cake Order Book

DESIGN

Cake Order Book

ORDER NUMBER   ORDER DATE

PICKUP ☐   DELIVERY ☐   DELIVERY DATE

CUSTOMER DETAILS

NAME ....

ADDRESS ....

PHONE NUMBER ....

E-MAIL ....

CAKE DETAILS

CAKE TYPE .... TIER ....

QUANTIFY .... CAKE SIZE ....

FLAVOR .... SHAPE ....

COLOR SCHEME .... FROSTING ....

FILLING .... WRITING ....

SPECIAL INSTRUCTIONS ....

....

....

NOTES

....

....

....

PAYMENT DETAILS

TOTAL   DEPOSIT   TOTAL
COST .... PAID .... PAID ....

FORM OF PAYMENT ....

Cake Order Book

DESIGN

Cake Order Book

ORDER NUMBER

ORDER DATE

PICKUP ☐   DELIVERY ☐

DELIVERY DATE

CUSTOMER DETAILS

NAME ....

ADDRESS ....

PHONE NUMBER ....

E-MAIL ....

CAKE DETAILS

CAKE TYPE .... TIER ....

QUANTIFY .... CAKE SIZE ....

FLAVOR .... SHAPE ....

COLOR SCHEME .... FROSTING ....

FILLING .... WRITING ....

SPECIAL INSTRUCTIONS ....

....

....

NOTES

....
....
....

PAYMENT DETAILS

TOTAL COST ....

DEPOSIT PAID ....

TOTAL PAID ....

FORM OF PAYMENT ....

Cake Order Book

DESIGN

....

....

....

....

....

....

....

....

....

....

Cake Order Book

ORDER NUMBER   ORDER DATE

PICKUP ☐   DELIVERY ☐   DELIVERY DATE

CUSTOMER DETAILS

NAME ....

ADDRESS ....

PHONE NUMBER ....

E-MAIL ....

CAKE DETAILS

CAKE TYPE .... **TIER** ....

QUANTIFY .... **CAKE SIZE** ....

FLAVOR .... **SHAPE** ....

COLOR SCHEME .... **FROSTING** ....

FILLING .... **WRITING** ....

SPECIAL INSTRUCTIONS ....

....

....

NOTES

....
....
....

PAYMENT DETAILS

TOTAL COST ....   **DEPOSIT PAID** ....   **TOTAL PAID** ....

FORM OF PAYMENT ....

Cake Order Book

....
....
....
....
....
....
....
....
....
....
....

Cake Order Book

ORDER NUMBER   ORDER DATE

PICKUP ☐   DELIVERY ☐   DELIVERY DATE

CUSTOMER DETAILS

NAME ....

ADDRESS ....

PHONE NUMBER ....

E-MAIL ....

CAKE DETAILS

CAKE TYPE .... TIER ....

QUANTIFY .... CAKE SIZE ....

FLAVOR .... SHAPE ....

COLOR SCHEME .... FROSTING ....

FILLING .... WRITING ....

SPECIAL INSTRUCTIONS ....

....

....

NOTES

....

....

....

PAYMENT DETAILS

TOTAL   DEPOSIT   TOTAL
COST ....   PAID ....   PAID ....

FORM OF PAYMENT ....

Cake Order Book

DESIGN

Cake Order Book

ORDER NUMBER   ORDER DATE

PICKUP ☐   DELIVERY ☐   DELIVERY DATE

CUSTOMER DETAILS

NAME ....

ADDRESS ....

PHONE NUMBER ....

E-MAIL ....

CAKE DETAILS

CAKE TYPE .... TIER ....

QUANTIFY .... CAKE SIZE ....

FLAVOR .... SHAPE ....

COLOR SCHEME .... FROSTING ....

FILLING .... WRITING ....

SPECIAL INSTRUCTIONS ....

....

....

NOTES

....
....
....

PAYMENT DETAILS

TOTAL   DEPOSIT   TOTAL
COST ....   PAID ....   PAID ....

FORM OF PAYMENT ....

Cake Order Book

DESIGN

....

....

....

....

....

....

....

....

....

....

Cake Order Book

ORDER NUMBER

ORDER DATE

PICKUP ☐   DELIVERY ☐   DELIVERY DATE

CUSTOMER DETAILS

NAME ....

ADDRESS ....

PHONE NUMBER ....

E-MAIL ....

CAKE DETAILS

CAKE TYPE ....   TIER ....

QUANTIFY ....   CAKE SIZE ....

FLAVOR ....   SHAPE ....

COLOR SCHEME ....   FROSTING ....

FILLING ....   WRITING ....

SPECIAL INSTRUCTIONS ....

....

....

NOTES

....

....

....

PAYMENT DETAILS

TOTAL COST ....   DEPOSIT PAID ....   TOTAL PAID ....

FORM OF PAYMENT ....

Cake Order Book

....
....
....
....
....
....
....
....
....
....

Cake Order Book

ORDER NUMBER · ORDER DATE

PICKUP ☐   DELIVERY ☐   DELIVERY DATE

CUSTOMER DETAILS

NAME ....

ADDRESS ....

PHONE NUMBER ....

E-MAIL ....

CAKE DETAILS

CAKE TYPE .... TIER ....

QUANTIFY .... CAKE SIZE ....

FLAVOR .... SHAPE ....

COLOR SCHEME .... FROSTING ....

FILLING .... WRITING ....

SPECIAL INSTRUCTIONS ....

....

....

NOTES

....
....
....

PAYMENT DETAILS

TOTAL   DEPOSIT   TOTAL
COST ....   PAID ....   PAID ....

FORM OF PAYMENT ....

Cake Order Book

DESIGN

....
....
....
....
....
....
....
....
....

Cake Order Book

ORDER NUMBER   ORDER DATE

PICKUP ☐   DELIVERY ☐   DELIVERY DATE

CUSTOMER DETAILS

NAME ....

ADDRESS ....

PHONE NUMBER ....

E-MAIL ....

CAKE DETAILS

CAKE TYPE ....   TIER ....

QUANTIFY ....   CAKE SIZE ....

FLAVOR ....   SHAPE ....

COLOR SCHEME ....   FROSTING ....

FILLING ....   WRITING ....

SPECIAL INSTRUCTIONS ....

....

....

NOTES

....
....
....

PAYMENT DETAILS

TOTAL   DEPOSIT   TOTAL
COST .... PAID ....   PAID ....

FORM OF PAYMENT ....

Cake Order Book

DESIGN

....
....
....
....
....
....
....
....
....
....

Cake Order Book

ORDER NUMBER .... ORDER DATE ....

PICKUP ☐   DELIVERY ☐   DELIVERY DATE ....

CUSTOMER DETAILS

NAME ....

ADDRESS ....

PHONE NUMBER ....

E-MAIL ....

CAKE DETAILS

CAKE TYPE ....   **TIER** ....

QUANTIFY ....   **CAKE SIZE** ....

FLAVOR ....   **SHAPE** ....

COLOR SCHEME ....   **FROSTING** ....

FILLING ....   **WRITING** ....

SPECIAL INSTRUCTIONS ....

....

....

NOTES

....

....

....

PAYMENT DETAILS

TOTAL COST ....   **DEPOSIT PAID** ....   **TOTAL PAID** ....

FORM OF PAYMENT ....

Cake Order Book

DESIGN

....
....
....
....
....
....
....
....
....
....

Cake Order Book

ORDER NUMBER   **ORDER DATE**

PICKUP ☐   **DELIVERY** ☐   **DELIVERY DATE**

CUSTOMER DETAILS

NAME ....

ADDRESS ....

PHONE NUMBER ....

E-MAIL ....

CAKE DETAILS

CAKE TYPE .... **TIER** ....

QUANTIFY .... **CAKE SIZE** ....

FLAVOR .... **SHAPE** ....

COLOR SCHEME .... **FROSTING** ....

FILLING .... **WRITING** ....

SPECIAL INSTRUCTIONS ....

....

....

NOTES

....

....

....

PAYMENT DETAILS

TOTAL COST ....   **DEPOSIT PAID** ....   **TOTAL PAID** ....

FORM OF PAYMENT ....

Cake Order Book

DESIGN

....
....
....
....
....
....
....
....
....
....
....

Cake Order Book

ORDER NUMBER .... ORDER DATE ....

PICKUP ☐   DELIVERY ☐   DELIVERY DATE ....

CUSTOMER DETAILS

NAME ....

ADDRESS ....

PHONE NUMBER ....

E-MAIL ....

CAKE DETAILS

CAKE TYPE .... TIER ....

QUANTIFY .... CAKE SIZE ....

FLAVOR .... SHAPE ....

COLOR SCHEME .... FROSTING ....

FILLING .... WRITING ....

SPECIAL INSTRUCTIONS ....

....

....

NOTES

....
....
....

PAYMENT DETAILS

TOTAL   DEPOSIT   TOTAL
COST ....   PAID ....   PAID ....

FORM OF PAYMENT ....

Cake Order Book

....

....

....

....

....

....

....

....

....

....

Cake Order Book

ORDER NUMBER .... ORDER DATE ....

PICKUP ☐ DELIVERY ☐ DELIVERY DATE ....

CUSTOMER DETAILS

NAME ....

ADDRESS ....

PHONE NUMBER ....

E-MAIL ....

CAKE DETAILS

CAKE TYPE .... TIER ....

QUANTIFY .... CAKE SIZE ....

FLAVOR .... SHAPE ....

COLOR SCHEME .... FROSTING ....

FILLING .... WRITING ....

SPECIAL INSTRUCTIONS ....

....

....

NOTES

....

....

....

PAYMENT DETAILS

TOTAL COST .... DEPOSIT PAID .... TOTAL PAID ....

FORM OF PAYMENT ....

Cake Order Book

DESIGN

....
....
....
....
....
....
....
....
....
....
....

Cake Order Book

ORDER NUMBER   ORDER DATE

PICKUP ☐   DELIVERY ☐   DELIVERY DATE

CUSTOMER DETAILS

NAME ....

ADDRESS ....

PHONE NUMBER ....

E-MAIL ....

CAKE DETAILS

CAKE TYPE ....   **TIER** ....

QUANTIFY ....   **CAKE SIZE** ....

FLAVOR ....   **SHAPE** ....

COLOR SCHEME ....   **FROSTING** ....

FILLING ....   **WRITING** ....

SPECIAL INSTRUCTIONS ....

....

....

NOTES

....
....
....

PAYMENT DETAILS

TOTAL COST ....   **DEPOSIT PAID** ....   **TOTAL PAID** ....

FORM OF PAYMENT ....

Cake Order Book

DESIGN

....
....
....
....
....
....
....
....
....
....

Cake Order Book

ORDER NUMBER   ORDER DATE

PICKUP ☐   DELIVERY ☐   DELIVERY DATE

CUSTOMER DETAILS

NAME ....

ADDRESS ....

PHONE NUMBER ....

E-MAIL ....

CAKE DETAILS

CAKE TYPE ....   TIER ....

QUANTIFY ....   CAKE SIZE ....

FLAVOR ....   SHAPE ....

COLOR SCHEME ....   FROSTING ....

FILLING ....   WRITING ....

SPECIAL INSTRUCTIONS ....

....

....

NOTES

....

....

....

PAYMENT DETAILS

TOTAL   DEPOSIT   TOTAL
COST ....   PAID ....   PAID ....

FORM OF PAYMENT ....

Cake Order Book

DESIGN

....
....
....
....
....
....
....
....
....
....
....

Cake Order Book

ORDER NUMBER   ORDER DATE

PICKUP ☐   DELIVERY ☐   DELIVERY DATE

CUSTOMER DETAILS

NAME ....

ADDRESS ....

PHONE NUMBER ....

E-MAIL ....

CAKE DETAILS

CAKE TYPE ....   **TIER** ....

QUANTIFY ....   **CAKE SIZE** ....

FLAVOR ....   **SHAPE** ....

COLOR SCHEME ....   **FROSTING** ....

FILLING ....   **WRITING** ....

SPECIAL INSTRUCTIONS ....

....

....

NOTES

....
....
....

PAYMENT DETAILS

TOTAL COST ....   **DEPOSIT PAID** ....   **TOTAL PAID** ....

FORM OF PAYMENT ....

Cake Order Book

DESIGN

....
....
....
....
....
....
....
....
....
....
....

Cake Order Book

ORDER NUMBER .... ORDER DATE ....

PICKUP ☐ DELIVERY ☐ DELIVERY DATE ....

CUSTOMER DETAILS

NAME ....

ADDRESS ....

PHONE NUMBER ....

E-MAIL ....

CAKE DETAILS

CAKE TYPE .... TIER ....

QUANTIFY .... CAKE SIZE ....

FLAVOR .... SHAPE ....

COLOR SCHEME .... FROSTING ....

FILLING .... WRITING ....

SPECIAL INSTRUCTIONS ....

....

....

NOTES

....

....

....

PAYMENT DETAILS

TOTAL COST .... DEPOSIT PAID .... TOTAL PAID ....

FORM OF PAYMENT ....

Cake Order Book

DESIGN

Cake Order Book

ORDER NUMBER

ORDER DATE

PICKUP ☐   DELIVERY ☐

DELIVERY DATE

CUSTOMER DETAILS

NAME ....

ADDRESS ....

PHONE NUMBER ....

E-MAIL ....

CAKE DETAILS

CAKE TYPE .... **TIER** ....

QUANTIFY .... **CAKE SIZE** ....

FLAVOR .... **SHAPE** ....

COLOR SCHEME .... **FROSTING** ....

FILLING .... **WRITING** ....

SPECIAL INSTRUCTIONS ....

....

....

NOTES

....

....

....

PAYMENT DETAILS

TOTAL COST ....   **DEPOSIT PAID** ....   **TOTAL PAID** ....

FORM OF PAYMENT ....

Cake Order Book

DESIGN

....
....
....
....
....
....
....
....
....
....
....

Cake Order Book

ORDER NUMBER .... ORDER DATE ....

PICKUP ☐   DELIVERY ☐   DELIVERY DATE

CUSTOMER DETAILS

NAME ....

ADDRESS ....

PHONE NUMBER ....

E-MAIL ....

CAKE DETAILS

CAKE TYPE ....   TIER ....

QUANTIFY ....   CAKE SIZE ....

FLAVOR ....   SHAPE ....

COLOR SCHEME ....   FROSTING ....

FILLING ....   WRITING ....

SPECIAL INSTRUCTIONS ....

....

....

NOTES

....

....

....

PAYMENT DETAILS

TOTAL   DEPOSIT   TOTAL
COST ....   PAID ....   PAID ....

FORM OF PAYMENT ....

Cake Order Book

DESIGN

....

....

....

....

....

....

....

....

Cake Order Book

ORDER NUMBER _____ ORDER DATE _____

PICKUP ☐   DELIVERY ☐   DELIVERY DATE _____

CUSTOMER DETAILS

NAME ....

ADDRESS ....

PHONE NUMBER ....

E-MAIL ....

CAKE DETAILS

CAKE TYPE .... TIER ....

QUANTIFY .... CAKE SIZE ....

FLAVOR .... SHAPE ....

COLOR SCHEME .... FROSTING ....

FILLING .... WRITING ....

SPECIAL INSTRUCTIONS ....

....

....

NOTES

....

....

....

PAYMENT DETAILS

TOTAL COST ....   DEPOSIT PAID ....   TOTAL PAID ....

FORM OF PAYMENT ....

Cake Order Book

DESIGN

···
···
···
···
···
···
···
···
···
···

Cake Order Book

ORDER NUMBER .... ORDER DATE ....

PICKUP ☐   DELIVERY ☐   DELIVERY DATE

CUSTOMER DETAILS

NAME ....

ADDRESS ....

PHONE NUMBER ....

E-MAIL ....

CAKE DETAILS

CAKE TYPE .... **TIER** ....

QUANTIFY .... **CAKE SIZE** ....

FLAVOR .... **SHAPE** ....

COLOR SCHEME .... **FROSTING** ....

FILLING .... **WRITING** ....

SPECIAL INSTRUCTIONS ....

....

....

NOTES

....
....
....

PAYMENT DETAILS

TOTAL COST ....   **DEPOSIT PAID** ....   **TOTAL PAID** ....

FORM OF PAYMENT ....

Cake Order Book

DESIGN

....
....
....
....
....
....
....
....
....
....

Cake Order Book

ORDER NUMBER   ORDER DATE

PICKUP ☐   DELIVERY ☐   DELIVERY DATE

CUSTOMER DETAILS

NAME ....

ADDRESS ....

PHONE NUMBER ....

E-MAIL ....

CAKE DETAILS

CAKE TYPE .... TIER ....

QUANTIFY .... CAKE SIZE ....

FLAVOR .... SHAPE ....

COLOR SCHEME .... FROSTING ....

FILLING .... WRITING ....

SPECIAL INSTRUCTIONS ....

....

....

NOTES

....
....
....

PAYMENT DETAILS

TOTAL   DEPOSIT   TOTAL
COST   ....   PAID   ....   PAID   ....

FORM OF PAYMENT ....

Cake Order Book

DESIGN

Cake Order Book

ORDER NUMBER .... ORDER DATE ....

PICKUP ☐ DELIVERY ☐   DELIVERY DATE ....

CUSTOMER DETAILS

NAME ....

ADDRESS ....

PHONE NUMBER ....

E-MAIL ....

CAKE DETAILS

CAKE TYPE .... TIER ....

QUANTIFY .... CAKE SIZE ....

FLAVOR .... SHAPE ....

COLOR SCHEME .... FROSTING ....

FILLING .... WRITING ....

SPECIAL INSTRUCTIONS ....

....

....

NOTES

....

....

....

PAYMENT DETAILS

TOTAL   DEPOSIT   TOTAL
COST ....   PAID ....   PAID ....

FORM OF PAYMENT ....

Cake Order Book

....
....
....
....
....
....
....
....
....
....

Cake Order Book

ORDER NUMBER   ORDER DATE

PICKUP ☐   DELIVERY ☐   DELIVERY DATE

CUSTOMER DETAILS

NAME ....

ADDRESS ....

PHONE NUMBER ....

E-MAIL ....

CAKE DETAILS

CAKE TYPE .... **TIER** ....

QUANTIFY .... **CAKE SIZE** ....

FLAVOR .... **SHAPE** ....

COLOR SCHEME .... **FROSTING** ....

FILLING .... **WRITING** ....

SPECIAL INSTRUCTIONS ....

....

....

NOTES

....

....

....

PAYMENT DETAILS

TOTAL COST ....   **DEPOSIT PAID** ....   **TOTAL PAID** ....

FORM OF PAYMENT ....

Cake Order Book

....

....

....

....

....

....

....

....

....

....

Cake Order Book

ORDER NUMBER .... ORDER DATE ....

PICKUP ☐   DELIVERY ☐   DELIVERY DATE ....

CUSTOMER DETAILS

NAME ....

ADDRESS ....

PHONE NUMBER ....

E-MAIL ....

CAKE DETAILS

CAKE TYPE .... **TIER** ....

QUANTIFY .... **CAKE SIZE** ....

FLAVOR .... **SHAPE** ....

COLOR SCHEME .... **FROSTING** ....

FILLING .... **WRITING** ....

SPECIAL INSTRUCTIONS ....

....

....

NOTES

....

....

....

PAYMENT DETAILS

TOTAL COST ....   **DEPOSIT PAID** ....   **TOTAL PAID** ....

FORM OF PAYMENT ....

Cake Order Book

....

....

....

....

....

....

....

....

....

....

....

Cake Order Book

ORDER NUMBER .... ORDER DATE ....

PICKUP ☐   DELIVERY ☐   DELIVERY DATE

CUSTOMER DETAILS

NAME ....

ADDRESS ....

PHONE NUMBER ....

E-MAIL ....

CAKE DETAILS

CAKE TYPE .... TIER ....

QUANTIFY .... CAKE SIZE ....

FLAVOR .... SHAPE ....

COLOR SCHEME .... FROSTING ....

FILLING .... WRITING ....

SPECIAL INSTRUCTIONS ....

....

....

NOTES

....

....

....

PAYMENT DETAILS

TOTAL COST .... DEPOSIT PAID .... TOTAL PAID ....

FORM OF PAYMENT ....

Cake Order Book

DESIGN

....
....
....
....
....
....
....
....
....
....
....
....

Cake Order Book

ORDER NUMBER .... ORDER DATE ....

PICKUP ☐ DELIVERY ☐ DELIVERY DATE

CUSTOMER DETAILS

NAME ....

ADDRESS ....

PHONE NUMBER ....

E-MAIL ....

CAKE DETAILS

CAKE TYPE .... **TIER** ....

QUANTIFY .... **CAKE SIZE** ....

FLAVOR .... **SHAPE** ....

COLOR SCHEME .... **FROSTING** ....

FILLING .... **WRITING** ....

SPECIAL INSTRUCTIONS ....

....

....

NOTES

....

....

....

PAYMENT DETAILS

TOTAL COST ....   **DEPOSIT PAID** ....   **TOTAL PAID** ....

FORM OF PAYMENT ....

Cake Order Book

DESIGN

....
....
....
....
....
....
....
....
....
....

Made in the USA
Monee, IL
09 June 2021